What's this?!

Hi! I'm Julia.

I put a picture of a cat on the internet here:

✵ | jvns.ca/cat.png | ✵ (go look!)

In this zine, we'll learn everything (mostly) that needs to happen to get that cat picture from my server to your laptop.

My goal is to help get you from:

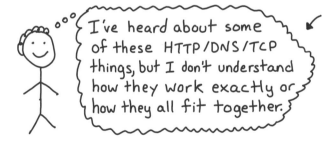

I've heard about some of these HTTP/DNS/TCP things, but I don't understand how they work exactly or how they all fit together.

← me after I'd been working as a web developer for a year

to...

there's a networking problem! I totally know where to start!

← me now

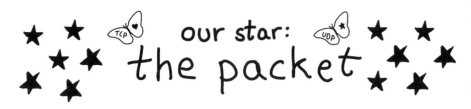

our star: the packet

All data is sent over the internet in {packets}. A packet is a series of bits (01101001...) and it's split into section (aka "headers").

Here's what a UDP packet that says "mangotea" looks like. It's 50 bytes (400 bits) in all!

Julia, I don't understand this diagram

We are going to work on explaining it!

◄———— 84 bits ————►

destination MAC	Source MAC addr	type

Ethernet frame header (14 bytes)

4 bytes
◄———— 32 bits ————►

ver	hlen	TOS	packet length	
identification		flg	fragment offst	
TTL	protocol		header checksum	
Source IP address				
Destination IP address				

IP header 160 bits / 20 bytes

This tells routers what IP to send the packet to.

source port	destination port
length	UDP checksum

UDP header 64 bits / 8 bytes
(a TCP packet would have a TCP header instead here)

m	a	n	g
o	t	e	a

The packet's "contents" go here. ASCII characters are 1 byte so "mangotea" = 8 bytes / 64 bits

steps to get a cat picture

from jvns.ca/cat.png

When you download an image, there are a LOT of networking moving pieces. Here are the basic steps, which we'll explain in the next few pages.

① get the IP address for jvns.ca

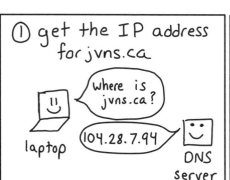

② open a {socket}

③ open a TCP connection to 104.28.7.94 port 80

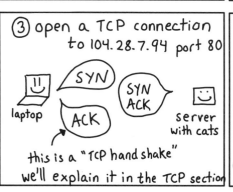

this is a "TCP handshake" we'll explain it in the TCP section

④ request a cat

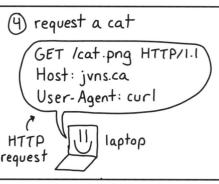

⑤ get a cat back

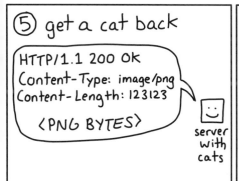

⑥ clean up

-> close the connection, maybe

-> put the bytes for the PNG in a file, maybe

-> look at cats, definitely.

DNS

All networking happens by sending packets. To send a packet to a server on the internet, you need an ⟨IP address⟩ like 104.28.7.94.

jvns.ca and google.com are domain names. DNS (the "Domain Name System") is the protocol we use to get the IP address for a domain name.

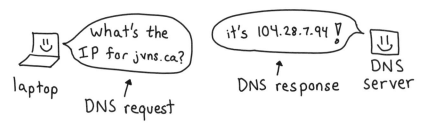

what's the IP for jvns.ca?

laptop

DNS request

it's 104.28.7.94 !

DNS response

DNS server

The DNS request & response are both usually UDP packets.

When you run $ curl jvns.ca/cat.png:

curl calls the getaddrinfo function with jvns.ca	getaddrinfo finds the system DNS server (like 8.8.8.8)	getaddrinfo makes a DNS request to 8.8.8.8	IP address: ★ obtained! ★ 104.28.7.94

Your system's default DNS server is often configured in /etc/resolv.conf.

8.8.8.8 is Google's DNS server, and lots of people use it. Try it if your default DNS server isn't working!

There are 2 kinds of DNS servers:

recursive

DNS — I can get you an IP address for ANY website by asking the right authoritative server.

authoritative

DNS server (like art.ns.cloudflare.com) — wanna know where jvns.ca is? Talk to ME!

When you query a recursive DNS server, here's what happens:

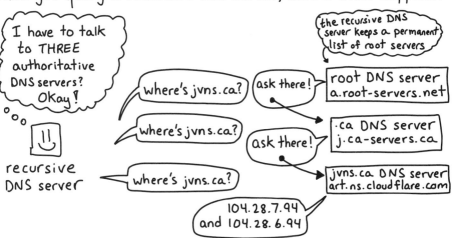

I have to talk to THREE authoritative DNS servers? Okay!

recursive DNS server

where's jvns.ca? — ask there!

where's jvns.ca? — ask there!

where's jvns.ca?

the recursive DNS server keeps a permanent list of root servers

root DNS server a.root-servers.net

.ca DNS server j.ca-servers.ca

jvns.ca DNS server art.ns.cloudflare.com

104.28.7.94 and 104.28.6.94

Recursive DNS servers usually cache DNS records. Every DNS record has a TTL ("time to live") that says how long to cache it for. You often can't force them to update their cache. You just have to wait:

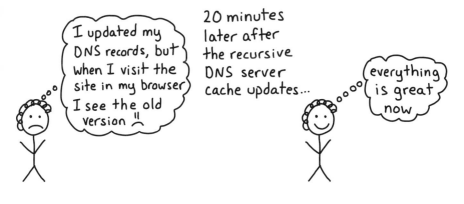

I updated my DNS records, but when I visit the site in my browser I see the old version ‼

20 minutes later after the recursive DNS server cache updates...

everything is great now

let's make ♡ DNS requests ♡

When you're setting up DNS for a new domain, often this happens:

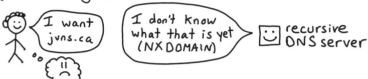

I want jvns.ca

I don't know what that is yet (NX DOMAIN)

recursive DNS server

Here's how you can make DNS queries from the command line to understand what's going on:

```
$ dig jvns.ca
```

```
;; ANSWER SECTION
jvns.ca 268 IN A 104.28.6.94
jvns.ca 268 IN A 104.28.7.94

;; SERVER 127.0.1.1#53
```

this record expires after 268 seconds

an "A" record is an IP address

there can be lots of IP addresses for one domain

the DNS server I'm using

```
$ dig @8.8.8.8 jvns.ca
```

8.8.8.8 is Google's recursive DNS server. @8.8.8.8 queries that instead of the default.

```
$ dig +trace jvns.ca
```

```
      .  502441  IN NS h.root-servers.net
    ca. 172800  IN NS c.ca-servers.net
jvns.ca. 86400  IN NS art.ns.cloudflare.com
jvns.ca. 300    IN A 104.28.6.94
```

root DNS server!

these are the 3 authoritative servers an authoritative server has to query to get an IP for jvns.ca

dig +trace basically does the same thing a recursive DNS server would do to find your domain's IP.

sockets

Step ②: Now that we have an IP address, the next step is to open a socket! Let's learn what that is.

---

your program doesn't know how to do TCP

"idk what "TCP" is. I just want to get a web page"

OS

code.py
Program

"don't worry! I can help!"

---

what using sockets is like

step 1: ask the OS for a socket

step 2: <u>connect</u> the socket to an IP address and port

step 3: <u>write</u> to the socket to send data

---

4 common socket types

{TCP}
to use TCP

{UDP}
to use UDP

{raw}
for ULTIMATE POWER. ping uses this to send ICMP packets.

{unix}
to talk to programs on the same computer

When you <u>connect</u> with a TCP socket

OS

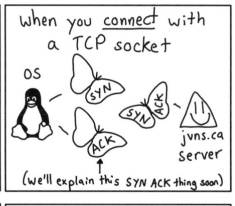

jvns.ca Server

SYN SYN ACK ACK

(we'll explain this SYN ACK thing soon)

When you <u>write</u> to a socket

code.py
program

-> writes lots of data ♥♥♥♥♥

splits it up
→ into packets to send it

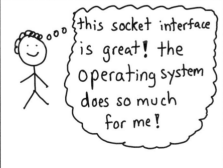

"this socket interface is great! the operating system does so much for me!"

TCP: how to reliably get a cat

Step 3 in our plan is "open a TCP connection!"
Let's learn what this "TCP" thing even is ☺

When you send a packet, sometimes it gets lost

jvns.ca server • Cat packets • "nope never got it" • laptop

TCP lets you send a stream of data reliably, even if packets get lost or sent in the wrong order.

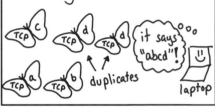

it says "abcd"! • duplicates • laptop

how does TCP work, you ask? WELL!

how to know what order the packets should go in:

    Every packet says what <u>range of bytes</u> it has.
    Like this:

once upon a ti	← bytes 0-13
agical oyster	← bytes 30-42
me there was a m	← bytes 14-29

Then the client can assemble all the pieces into:

"once upon a time there was a magical oyster"

The position of the first byte (0, 14, 30 in our example) is called the "sequence number".

how to deal with lost packets:

When you get TCP data, you have to acknowledge it (ACK):

jvns.ca server • here is part of a cat picture ! that should be 28832 bytes so far ! • yay • ACK! I have received all 28832 bytes • laptop

If the server doesn't get an ACKnowledgement, it will <u>retry</u> sending the data.

The TCP handshake

This is what a TCP header looks like:

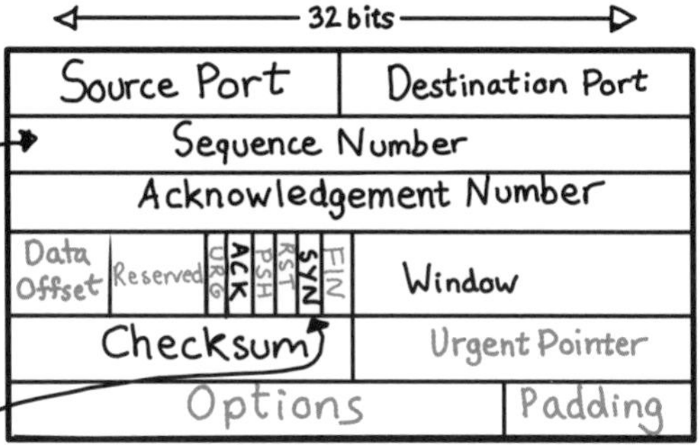

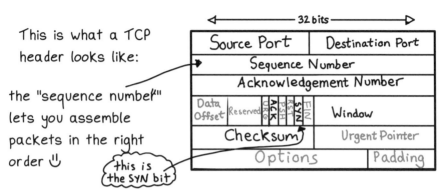

32 bits
Source Port
Destination Port
Sequence Number
Acknowledgement Number
Data Offset
Reserved
URG
ACK
PSH
RST
SYN
FIN
Window
Checksum
Urgent Pointer
Options
Padding

the "sequence number" lets you assemble packets in the right order ☺

this is the SYN bit

Every TCP connection starts with a "handshake". This makes sure both sides of the connection can communicate with each other.

SYN
SYN
ACK
ACK
client
server

But what do "SYN" and "ACK" mean? Well! TCP headers have 6 single bit flags (SYN, ACK, RST, FIN, PSH, URG) that you can set (you can see them in the diagram). A SYN packet is a packet with the SYN flag set to 1.

When you see "connection refused" or "connection timeout" errors, that means the TCP handshake didn't finish!
Here's what a TCP handshake looks like in tcpdump:

```
$ sudo tcpdump host jvns.ca
 localhost:51104 > 104.28.6.94:80  Flags [S]
 104.28.6.94:80 > localhost:51104  Flags [S.]
 localhost:51104 > 104.28.6.94:80  Flags [.]
```

TCP handshake!

jvns.ca IP address

S is for SYN
. is for ACK

HTTP

Step 4: Finally we can request cat.png!

Every time you get a webpage or see an image online, you're using HTTP.

HTTP is a pretty simple plaintext protocol. In fact, it's so simple that you can make an HTTP request by hand right now. Let's do it !!!

```
$ printf "GET / HTTP/1.1\r\nHost:      ⎫ one line
          example.com\r\n\r\n"          ⎬
       | nc example.com 80              ⎭
```

the `nc` command ("netcat") sets up a TCP connection to example.com and sends the HTTP request you wrote! The response we get back looks like:

```
200 OK
Content-Length: 120321
... headers ...

<html>
<body>
.... more HTML
```

I've heard of HTTP/2, what's that?

HTTP/2 is the next version of HTTP. Some big differences are that it's a binary protocol, you can make multiple requests at the same time, and you have to use TLS.

important HTTP headers

This is an HTTP request:

```
GET /cat.png HTTP/1.1
Host: jvns.ca
User-Agent: zine
```

The User-Agent and Host lines are called "headers".

They give the webserver extra information about what webpage you want!

{the Host header} ← my favorite!

GET /

GET /
Host: jvns.ca

dude, do you even know how many websites I serve? You gotta be more specific.

jvns.ca
Server

{NOW we're talking}

Most servers serve lots of different websites. The Host header lets you pick the one you want!

Servers also send response headers with extra information about the response.

More useful headers:

{User-Agent}

Lots of servers use this to check if you're using an old browser or if you're a bot.

{Accept-Encoding}

Want to save bandwidth? Set this to "gzip" and the server might compress your response.

{Cookie}

When you're logged into a website, your browser sends data in this header! This is how the server knows you're logged in.

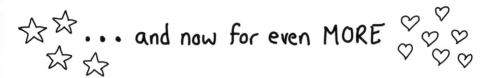

... and now for even MORE

We've covered the basics of how to download a cat picture now! But there's a lot more to know!
Let's talk about a few more topics.

We'll explain a little more about networking protocols:

→ what a port actually is
→ how a packet is put together
→ security: how SSL works
→ the different networking layers
→ UDP and why it's amazing

and how packets get sent from place to place:

→ how packets get sent in a local network
→ and how packets get from your house to jvns.ca
→ networking notation

let's learn MORE!

networking layers

I don't always find this useful, but it's good to know what "layer 4" means.

Networking layers mostly correspond to different sections of a packet.

Layer 1: wires + radio waves

Layer 2: Ethernet/wifi protocol
Your network card understands it.

Layer 3: IP addresses
routers look at this to decide where to send the packet next

Layer 4: TCP or UDP
Where you get your ports!

Layer 5+6: don't really exist (though they call SSL "layer 5")

Layer 7: HTTP and friends
Routers ignore this layer, mostly. DNS queries, emails, etc. go here.

— 84 bits —

destination MAC	source MAC addr	type

4 bytes
— 32 bits —

ver	hlen	TOS	packet length
identification		flg	fragment offst
TTL	protocol	header checksum	
Source IP address			
Destination IP address			

source port	destination port
length	UDP checksum

G	E	T	
/		H	T

layer 3 networking tool

↑
ignores layer 4 and above

I only know about IP addresses! I don't even know what a port is let alone what the packet says.

The cool thing is that the layers are mostly independent of each other - you can change the IP address (layer 3) and not worry about layers 4+7.

who uses which layer?

network card- layers 1+2
home router - layers 2+3+4
applications - mostly layer 7 but also layer 4 for the port

what's a :port: ?

ports are part of the TCP and UDP protocols.
(TCP port 999 and UDP port 999 are different!)
When you send a TCP message, you want to talk
to a specific kind of program.
This would be bad:

We want to have different kinds of programs on
the same server: {minecraft} {DNS} {email}

So every TCP/UDP packet has a port number
between 1 and 65535 on it:

netstat and lsof can tell you which ports are in use on your computer

some common ports	
DNS:	UDP port 53
HTTP:	TCP port 80
HTTPS:	TCP port 443
SMTP:	TCP port 25
Minecraft:	TCP + UDP port 25565

UDP

user datagram protocol

DNS sends requests using UDP. UDP is a really simple protocol. The packets look like this:

~ IP stuff ~   UDP header

source port	destination port
length	UDP checksum

~ packet contents ~

"unreliable data protocol"
(not what it really stands for)

When you send UDP packets, they might arrive:

- out of order
- never

<u>any</u> packet can actually get lost, but UDP won't do anything to help you.

Packet sizes are limited

I'm gonna put 3000 characters in this packet

nope, that won't fit. 1500 bytes is probably a better size. *

* packet sizes are actually a super interesting topic. Search "MTU".

you need to decide how to organize your data into packets manually

ok, 623 bytes in this packet, 747 bytes in that one...

VPNs use UDP

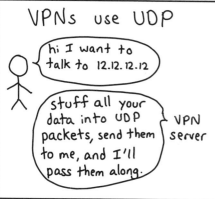

hi I want to talk to 12.12.12.12

stuff all your data into UDP packets, send them to me, and I'll pass them along.

VPN server

Streaming video often uses UDP

Read http://hpbn.co/webrtc for a GREAT discussion of using UDP in a real-time protocol.

Local networking

aka "how to talk to a computer in the same room"

Every computer is in a <u>subnet</u>. Your subnet is the list of computers that you can talk to directly.

What does it mean to talk "directly" to another computer? Well, every computer on the internet has a network card with a MAC address.

hello! you can call me
0a:58:ff:ea:05:97

network card

MAC address

Your laptop's IP address changes if you go to an internet cafe, but its MAC doesn't.

When you send a packet to a computer in your subnet, you put the computer's MAC address on it. To get the right MAC, your computer uses a protocol called ARP: "Address Resolution Protocol".

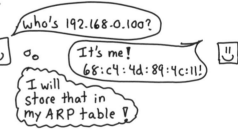

who's 192.168.0.100?

It's me!
68:c4:4d:89:4c:11!

I will store that in my ARP table!

You can run `arp -na` to see the contents of the ARP table on your computer. It should look like this:

MAC for 192.168.1.120 (my printer)

my wifi card

```
$ arp -na
? (192.168.1.120) at 94:53:30:30:91:98:c8 [ether] on wlp3s0
```

How packets get sent across the ocean

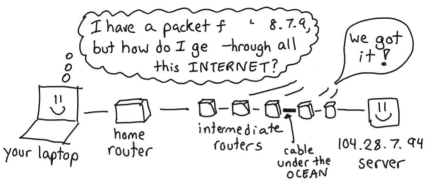

When a packet arrives at a router:

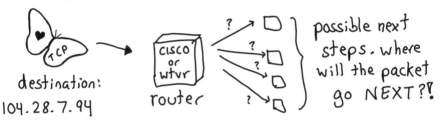

destination:
104.28.7.94

router

possible next steps. where will the packet go NEXT?!

Routers use a protocol called {BGP} to decide what router the packet should go to next:

A packet can take a lot of different routes to get to the same destination!

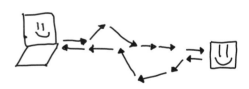

The route it takes to get from A→B might be different from B→A.

Exercise:

Run `traceroute google.com` to see what steps your packet takes to get to google.com.

Notation time!

$\{$ 10.0.0.0/8 $\}$ $\{$ 132.5.23.0/24 $\}$

People often describe groups of IP addresses using
CIDR notation.

$\{$ example CIDRs $\}$ $\{$ important examples $\}$

CIDR	range of IPs
10.0.0.0/8	10.*.*.*
10.9.0.0/16	10.9.*.*
10.9.8.0/24	10.9.8.*

10.0.0.0/8 and 192.168.0.0/16
and 172.16.0.0/12 are reserved
for local networking.

In CIDR notation, a /n gives you 2^{32-n}
IP addresses. So a /24 is $2^8 = 256$ IPs.

It's important to represent groups of IP addresses
efficiently because routers have LOTS TO DO.

router o oo $\{$ is 192.168.3.2 in the subnet
192.168.0.0/16? I can do some
really fast bit arithmetic and
find out! $\}$

The IP address 10.9.0.0 is this in binary:
10 ↘00001010 9 ↘00001001 0 ↘0000000 0 ↘00000000

‿‿‿‿‿‿‿‿‿‿‿‿‿‿
first 24 bits

10.9.0.0/24 is all the IP addresses which have the same
first 24 bits as 10.9.0.0!

SSL/TLS

(TLS: newer version of SSL)

When you send a packet on the internet, LOTS of people can potentially read it.

Unencrypted wifi

that person is sending email with pie recipes. HMMM.

SSL encrypts your packets:

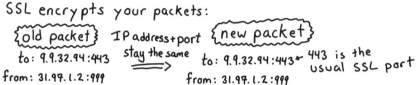

{old packet}
to: 9.9.32.94:443
from: 31.97.1.2:999

IP address+port stay the same ⟹

{new packet}
to: 9.9.32.94:443 ← 443 is the usual SSL port
from: 31.97.1.2:999

here is my secret lemon pie recipe ⟹ x8; fae94aex jjb43, 8b"5jkk ← nobody's gonna know the secret pie recipe NOW!

What happens when you go to https://jvns.ca:

hello — client

server — here's my SSL certificate / my half of the key exchange

here's my half of the key exchange — client

sweet. — server

(very simplified)

Once the client and server agree on a key for the session, they can encrypt all the communication they want.

To see the certificate for jvns.ca, run:

```
$ openssl s_client -connect jvns.ca:443 -servername jvns.ca
```

TLS is really complicated. You can use a tool like SSL Labs to check the security of your site.

wireshark

Wireshark is an *(amazing)* tool for packet analysis. Here's an exercise to learn it! Run this:

```
$ sudo tcpdump port 80 -w http.pcap
```

While that's running, open metafilter.com in your browser. Then press Ctrl+C to stop tcpdump. Now we have a pcap! Open http.pcap with Wireshark.

Some questions you can try to answer:

① What HTTP headers did your browser sent to metafilter.com?
  (hint: search `frame contains "GET"`)

How many packets were exchanged with metafilter.com's server?
  (hint: search `ip.dst == 54.1.2.3`)

put the IP from `ping metafilter.com` here

Wireshark makes it easy to look at:

- ★ IP addresses and ports
- ★ SYNS and ACKs for TCP traffic
- ★ exactly what's happening with DNS requests
- ★ and so much more! It's a great way to poke around and learn.